# PUPPET PARADE

Easy-To-Make Imaginative Puppets
From Readily-Found Materials

by Imogene Forte

Incentive Publications, Inc.
Nashville, Tennessee

*Illustrated by Susan Eaddy*
*Cover by Terrence Donaldson*
*Edited by Jan Keeling*

ISBN 0-86530-152-2

# Table of Contents

# Sew-So

# Art Smart

# Appendix

# PUPPET PARADE

## *How To Use This Book*

Welcome to the imaginative world of puppetry!

This book will teach you how to make your own puppets. Here are some things you need to know before you begin:

. . . All of these puppets are easy to make. You don't need a lot of supplies for any of them, and you don't have to work very long before you have a finished product you can be proud of to add to your own puppet parade.

. . . Collect puppet-making supplies so they will be ready to use. Find a sturdy bag, box, or basket to hold your supplies. Use the Puppet Maker's Tool Kit on page viii to help you collect basic art supplies and puppet-making materials. Once you have organized your supplies you will be ready for puppet production.

. . . Look through this book to learn about the many kinds of puppets you can make and the creative ways they can be used. Decide on the kind of puppet you want to make and how you want to use it. Perhaps it will be a puppet to use in a play, a puppet to put in your room as a decoration, or a puppet to add to a puppet collection. You may decide to give a puppet as a special gift. Maybe you want to make a puppet just for fun!

. . . Always read the complete instructions first. Gather your materials and arrange your work space before you start to work, being sure to cover your work area with newspapers if you will be pasting or painting. It is a good idea to check with the grownups to make sure that your plans meet with their approval.

. . . Copy or trace puppet patterns. You can save them in a notebook or folder so they can be used again.

. . . Puppet making is a terrific partner or team activity. Working together and sharing your puppets with a friend adds to the fun!

So select a puppet project that interests you, use your imagination, and get set to enjoy making and using puppets in extraordinary ways.

Imogene Forte

# PUPPET MAKER'S TOOL KIT

*Begin collecting the things
you will need to make puppets.*

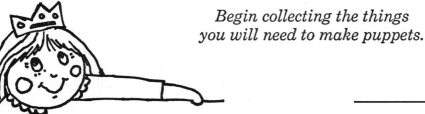

## Basic Art Supplies

- construction paper
- needle and thread
- typing paper       • crayons
- paste or glue      • tape
- newspaper          • paint
- tissue paper       • pencils
- tracing paper      • brads
- felt markers       • pins
- paintbrushes       • scissors

## Decorations

- photographs
- magazine pictures
- wrapping paper
- material scraps
- ribbon       • lace
- beads        • yarn
- buttons      • net
- seeds        • sequins
- string       • cotton

*Use your imagination
when collecting
puppet-making materials!*

## Puppet Materials

- cardboard           • styrofoam balls
- paper bags          • facial tissues
- paper plates        • plastic eggs
- paper cups          • modeling clay
- scarves             • dish scrubbers
- mopheads            • handkerchiefs
- playdough           • tissue paper rolls
- old socks, gloves, and mittens

## Tool Kit Containers

- egg cartons
    beads        • bags
    seeds        • sacks
    buttons      • boxes
- baskets

# FINGER FUN

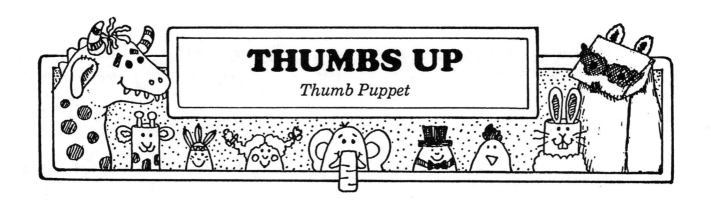

# THUMBS UP
*Thumb Puppet*

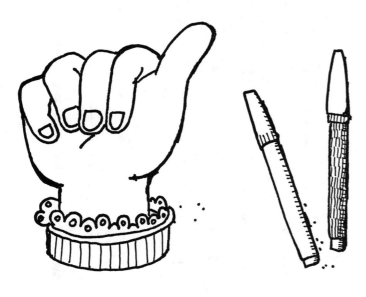

**What To Use:**

- your thumb
- washable felt tip pens

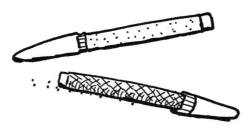

**What To Do:**

1. Make sure your thumb is clean.

2. Use the felt tip pens to draw eyes, nose, and a mouth on your thumb. You can use both of your thumbs to make it more fun!

# FANCY FINGERS

*Glove Finger Puppets*

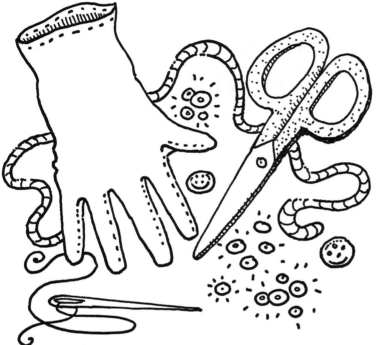

**What To Use:**

- old glove
- scissors
- "scrap box goodies" (beads, sequins, yarn, small buttons, etc.)
- needle and thread

**What To Do:**

1. Cut one of the fingers off the old glove.

2. Make a face on the cut-off glove finger by sewing on beads, sequins, yarn, small buttons, etc. You can wear finger puppets on the fingers of both hands and have them carry on conversations!

# TUBE TALK
*Paper Tube Puppets*

## What To Use:

- white paper
- tape
- felt tip pens
- colored paper, yarn, other trims

## What To Do:

1. Cut a strip of paper about as long as one of your fingers, and wide enough to fit around it. Wrap the paper around your finger to form a tube.

2. Form more paper tubes for more puppets.

3. Draw the faces of imaginative characters on the paper tubes with felt tip pens. Use colored paper, yarn, and other trims to make hats, ties, earrings, clothes, and other interesting add-ons.

4. When each tube is fully decorated, fasten the ends of the tube together with tape.

# ON A ROLL

*Tissue Paper Roll Puppet*

## What To Use:

- cardboard roll from toilet tissue
- construction paper
- scissors
- paste
- felt tip pens

## What To Do:

1. Cut the cardboard roll so it is a little longer than your longest finger. Cut construction paper and glue it around the roll.

2. Use felt tip pens to draw the face of your chosen character on the roll.

3. Add fringed strips of construction paper to make hair. Add other pieces of construction paper for paper hats, collars, neckties, skirts, and whatever else you like.

4. When it comes time to use your puppet, place two fingers inside the roll. If you want to do a play all by yourself, make puppets for both hands.

# TELL A TALE
*Wrap-Around Puppets*

Color the finger puppets on this page.

Cut them out and tape each one so it will wrap around a finger.

Write a play for the puppet characters.

Present your play.

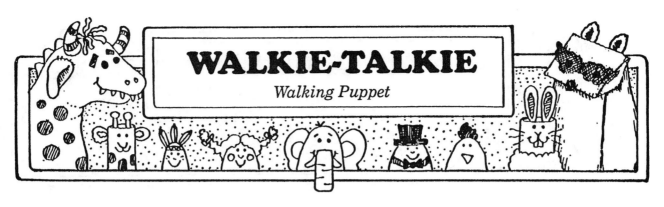

# WALKIE-TALKIE
*Walking Puppet*

## What To Use:

- magazines, old storybooks, or comic books
- cardboard
- scissors
- paste

## What To Do:

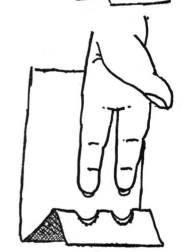

1. Choose a picture of a character from a magazine, old storybook, or comic book, and cut it out. If the picture shows the legs of the character, cut them off a little below the knees.

2. Cut out a cardboard rectangle 2 inches longer and a little wider than the character you have chosen.

3. Draw a line about 1 inch from the bottom edge of the cardboard, and another line about 1½ inches from the bottom edge. Fold the cardboard back on the first line, and forward on the second line (see illustration).

4. Cut 2 holes in the fold nearest the bottom edge, as shown. Ask an adult for help if you need it. Make sure the holes are large enough so you can put a finger through each one to make the legs of the puppet.

5. Paste the character cut-out to the cardboard, positioning it so that the knees just cover the fold as in the illustration. Cut out the cardboard around the outline of the character.

6. Put your fingers through the holes and make the puppet run, jump, and dance!

# SHOW AND TELL
*People Puppets*

Color and cut out the finger puppets below. Place one on each hand, sticking your fingers through the holes, and use the puppets to explain how to do one of the following activities:

1. How to wrap a package and tie it with a ribbon bow.
2. How to peel an apple and take the core out.
3. How to make a paper airplane and fly it.
4. How to build a rope swing and tie it from a tree branch.

Be sure the puppets do the talking!

*These puppets are also good for role play. Try having them act out "mannerly actions" or act out the answers to "What would you do if . . ." questions.*

17

# OLD FAVORITES

*Story Time Puppets*

## What To Use:

- scissors
- felt tip pens
- paste
- posterboard

## What To Do:

1. Color the finger puppets on the following 3 pages with felt tip pens.

2. Cut the puppets apart from one another. Paste each puppet to a piece of posterboard, then cut around the dotted lines. Ask an adult for help in cutting out the holes if you need it.

3. Put your fingers through the holes to make legs for your story puppets.

LITTLE RED RIDING ⇦ HOOD

The WOLF⇨

18

GRANDMA ⟵

THE WOOD-CUTTER

HANSEL ⟵

Gretel ⟹

19

WITCH
(for Hansel &
Gretel or
Rapunzel)

FATHER

PRINCE

RAPUNZEL

20

3 BILLY GOATS GRUFF

TROLL

21

# PAPER PALS
*Drawn Puppets*

## What To Use:

- white paper
- felt tip pens
- tape
- pencil

## What To Do:

1. Draw an imaginative character on white paper, making it "just the right size" to fit your finger.

2. Use felt tip pens to color and add interest to the puppet.

3. Cut out a strip of paper to fit around your finger and paste it to the character. Tape the ends of the paper together to form a tube that will slide over your finger.

happy

sad

surprised

angry

sleepy

puzzled

# PUPPET FACTORY

*Puppet Parts To Assemble*

Cut out the finger puppet form on this page. Select some of the parts illustrated below to make a funny, one-of-a-kind animal puppet. Color the parts, cut them out, and paste them onto the puppet form. Cut out the finger strip, glue it to the back of the puppet, and tape its ends together to make a tube to go on your finger.

Give your funny animal a name and write a puppet script telling about its habits and needs. Let your animal puppet present its story to the class.

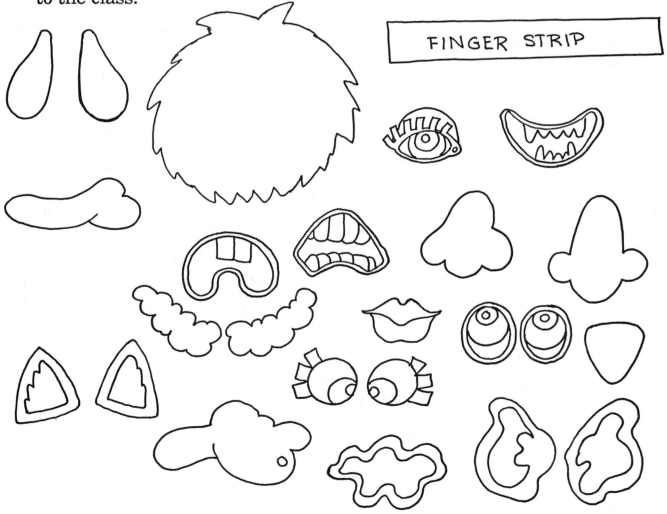

FINGER STRIP

24

# TOOLING AROUND

# CLEAR SAILING

*Sandwich Bag Puppet*

## What To Use:

- clear sandwich bag
- scissors
- glue or tape
- "scrap box goodies"

## What To Do:

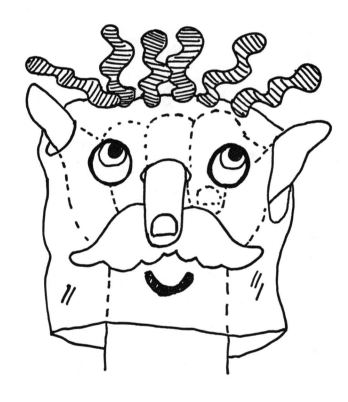

1. Cut 2 holes in the sides of the sandwich bag. Make them large enough for your thumb and little finger to poke through. These will be the puppet's arms.

2. Cut another hole in the center of the bag for the nose. You will put your middle finger through this hole.

3. Decorate your puppet by gluing or taping on "scrap box goodies" (yarn, felt or paper circles, etc.)

# CLEAN SWEEP

*Broom Puppet*

## What To Use:

- broom
- old pillowcase
- cloth strips
- felt tip pens or paints
- string
- scissors
- glue

## What To Do:

1. Slip the pillowcase over the broom bristles and tie it in place with a piece of string.

2. Cut strips of cloth and glue them into place for hair (rough heavy fabric from an old sweater or pair of jeans would make great hair).

3. Use felt tip pens or paints to give your broom puppet an amusing face.

*Life-size broom puppets make excellent dancing partners!*

# MOPPING UP
*Mophead Puppet*

**What To Use:**

- dust mop (without the handle)
- felt
- scissors
- glue

**What To Do:**

1. Remove the handle from the dust mop if it is still attached to the mophead.

2. Cut eyes, nose, and a mouth from felt. (Use newspaper to experiment with unusual shapes of features before cutting them in felt.)

3. Glue the features onto the mophead. Add a funny hat, head scarf, or wig if you have one.

*Two mophead puppets can be great fun for joke telling, riddles, or for use in a comical puppet play.*

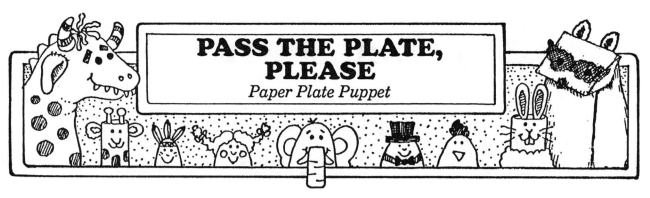

# PASS THE PLATE, PLEASE
*Paper Plate Puppet*

## What To Use:

- 2 paper plates
- paste or stapler
- crayons, felt tip pens, or paint
- scissors
- construction paper
- "scrap box goodies"

## What To Do:

1. Design a creative face on the back of one paper plate. Color, paint, or draw eyes, nose, and a mouth.

2. Cut the other paper plate in half. Paste or staple one of the halves to the top half of the "face plate" (the concave sides of the plates should be facing each other). This will make a space for your hand.

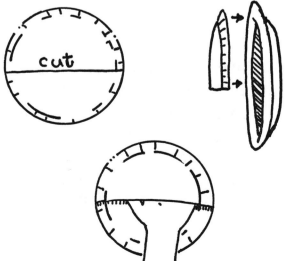

3. Finish your paper plate puppet by pasting on "scrap box goodies," construction paper ears, a hat, earrings, or other add-ons. If you like, you can make a small hole for the mouth. Stick your finger through the hole and wiggle it, and your puppet will have a tongue!

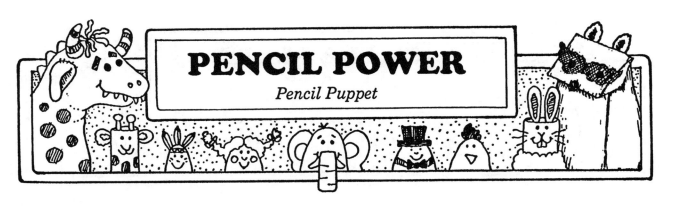

# PENCIL POWER

*Pencil Puppet*

## What To Use:

- tissue paper, white cloth, or handkerchief
- paper towels or facial tissues
- "scrap box goodies"

- pencil
- yarn
- felt tip pens

## What To Do:

1. Wrap some paper towels or tissues around the graphite end of the pencil.

2. Cover the padded pencil top with tissue paper, white cloth, or a handkerchief, and tie the covering tightly with yarn to form a "neck."

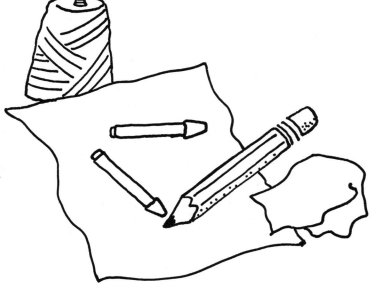

3. Draw eyes, nose, and mouth on the stuffed head with felt tip pens. Add yarn or string hair, buttons and bows, or other "scrap box goodies" to give your pencil puppet a one-of-a-kind personality.

# KITCHEN KAPERS

*Kitchen Tool Puppet*

**What To Use:**

- spatula or wooden spoon
- paper towel strips or scouring pads
- paste
- nuts, noodles, seeds

**What To Do:**

1. Find an old spatula or wooden spoon.

2. Make a face on the tool by pasting on nuts, noodles, seeds, etc. Add paper towel strips or scouring pads for hair if you like.

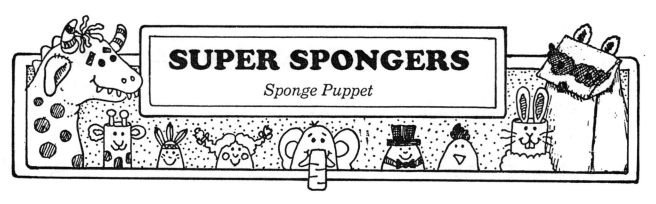

# SUPER SPONGERS

*Sponge Puppet*

## What To Use:

- "scrap box goodies"
- sponge
- glue
- pencil

## What To Do:

1. Glue "scrap box goodies" to sponge to make a face.

2. If your sponge is small, you may choose to simply hold your sponge puppet in your hand, or stick a pencil in the sponge and hold it by the pencil. If your sponge is

loofah sponge

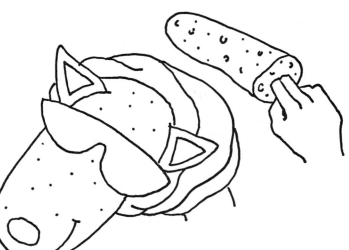

kitchen sponge

pipe cleaners

large and of a suitable shape, you may gouge out some holes in which to stick your fingers. To hide your hand, wrap a handkerchief or scarf around it.

3. To give your puppet some real character, add a hat, sunglasses, or a hair ribbon.

32

# MIRROR, MIRROR, WHO ARE YOU?
### Hand Mirror Puppet

## What To Use:

- hand mirror
- brown bag or wrapping paper
- paste
- yarn
- fabric scraps
- beads, buttons

## What To Do:

1. Paste brown paper to the back of a hand mirror. This will be the face of the puppet.

2. Decorate your puppet's face with yarn, fabric scraps, beads, buttons, etc., to give it a personality.

*Ask a friend to make a hand mirror puppet, too, and put on a play. Try to think of ways to use the mirror sides of the puppets. If you turn the mirrors toward the people in the audience, they can become characters in the play.*

33

# CUP TALK
*Paper Cup Puppets*

## What To Use:

- paper cup
- pencil
- construction paper
- felt tip pens
- paste
- buttons, sequins

## What To Do:

1. Use a sharpened pencil to punch two holes in the bottom of the cup. The holes should be large enough for your fingers.

2. Draw facial features on the cup with felt tip pens. Use construction paper to make a hat, hair, or other finishing touches. You can use the ideas on the following page for inspiration. Buttons and other trims from your scrap box can be used to add extra interest.

35

# HAPPY FACE

*Cereal Box Puppet*

## What To Use:

- empty individual-serving cereal box
- odds and ends from the scrap box (buttons, beads, felt scraps, etc.)
- tissue paper or gift wrap paper
- scissors
- paste

## What To Do:

1. Use the scissors to cut the box in half on three sides (see illustration).

2. Bend the box back on the uncut side to form the jaws of the puppet, as shown. Your thumb will go in one half of the box, your fingers in the other, to make the puppet "talk."

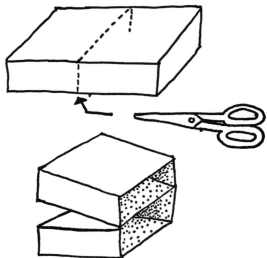

3. Cover the cereal box with construction paper and paste it in place.

4. Decorate your cereal box puppet with scraps of construction paper and other "scrap box goodies" to make a creature with personality!

# SEW-SO

# MITTEN MAGIC
*Simple Mitten Puppet*

## What To Use:

- old mitten
- needle and thread
- scrap of red fabric
- paste
- scissors
- 2 buttons
- cotton ball

## What To Do:

1. Cut the thumb off the mitten. Cut another hole approximately the same size on the opposite side of the mitten, as shown in the illustration.

2. Put a line of paste around each hole to keep it from unraveling.

3. Place the cotton ball inside the cut-off thumb to make the nose, and sew it in place.

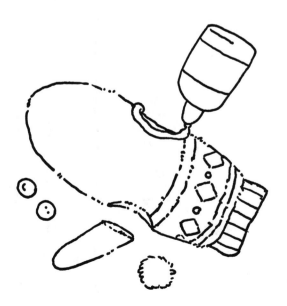

4. Make two marks where the eyes should go, and sew the buttons over them.

5. Make a mouth from the red fabric scrap and sew it in place.

6. Put your hand inside the transformed mitten. Your thumb and little finger will fit through the two side holes to make arms for your mitten puppet.

38

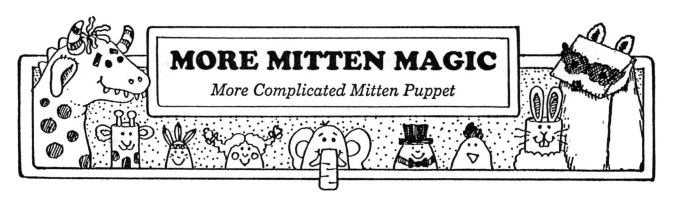

# MORE MITTEN MAGIC
*More Complicated Mitten Puppet*

## What To Use:

- mitten
- 2 buttons
- straight pins
- felt or fabric
- needle and thread

## What To Do:

1. Cut two ears and a nose out of felt or fabric, using the patterns on this page or making up your own.

2. Put the mitten on your hand and mark places for the eyes, nose, and ears. Notice that your thumb will be the lower jaw of the puppet. Sew the buttons over the eye markings, and the ears and nose in their proper places.

*Practice moving and bending your fingers and thumb inside the mitten to make your mitten puppet come alive!*

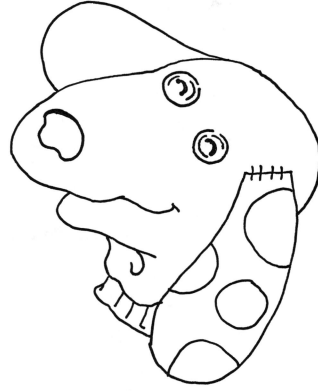

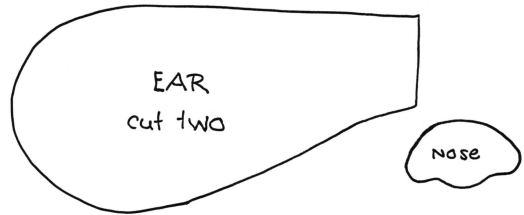

EAR
cut two

nose

39

# FACE-UP
*Footie Puppet*

## What To Use:

- old footie
- "scrap box goodies"
- needle and thread
- paste
- buttons

## What To Do:

1. Sew or paste scrap box goodies on the top or the bottom of a footie, creating a face that you like.

2. Place the footie over your hand and move your fingers to make different expressions as your puppet plays various roles.

# CHICK, CHICK, CHICKEN
*Felt Puppet*

## What To Use:

- felt squares:
    - 2 white for chicken body
    - 1 red for comb and wattle
    - 1 gold for bill
- scissors
- pencil
- needle and thread
- 2 buttons

## What To Do:

1. Cut out felt shapes, using the patterns on pages 42 and 43.

2. With right sides together, sew body pieces together as shown in illustration. Be sure to leave enough open space at the top to insert comb.

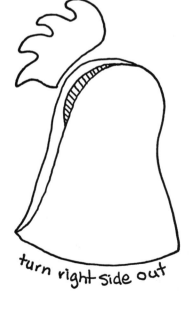

turn right side out

3. Turn puppet body right side out. Insert comb tab into opening and sew along seamline.

4. With right sides together, sew edges of bill together, leaving "tab" end open. Turn bill right side out and press flat, tucking tabs inside. Stitch these folded tab edges onto the chicken's face.

5. Stitch wattle under bill. For the eyes, sew on buttons as indicated on body pattern.

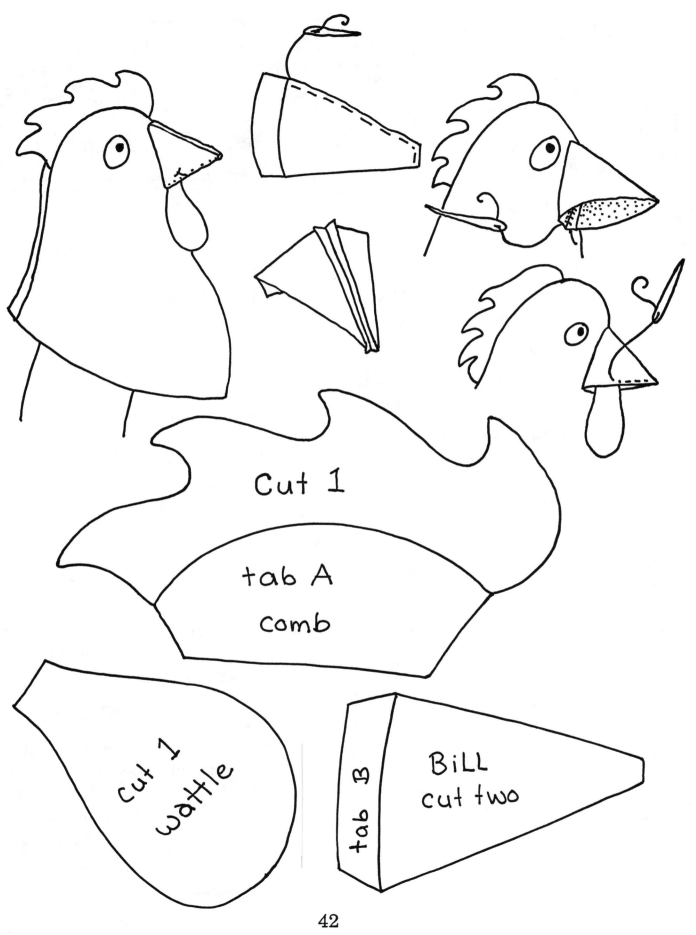

Cut 1

tab A
comb

cut 1
wattle

BiLL
cut two

tab B

42

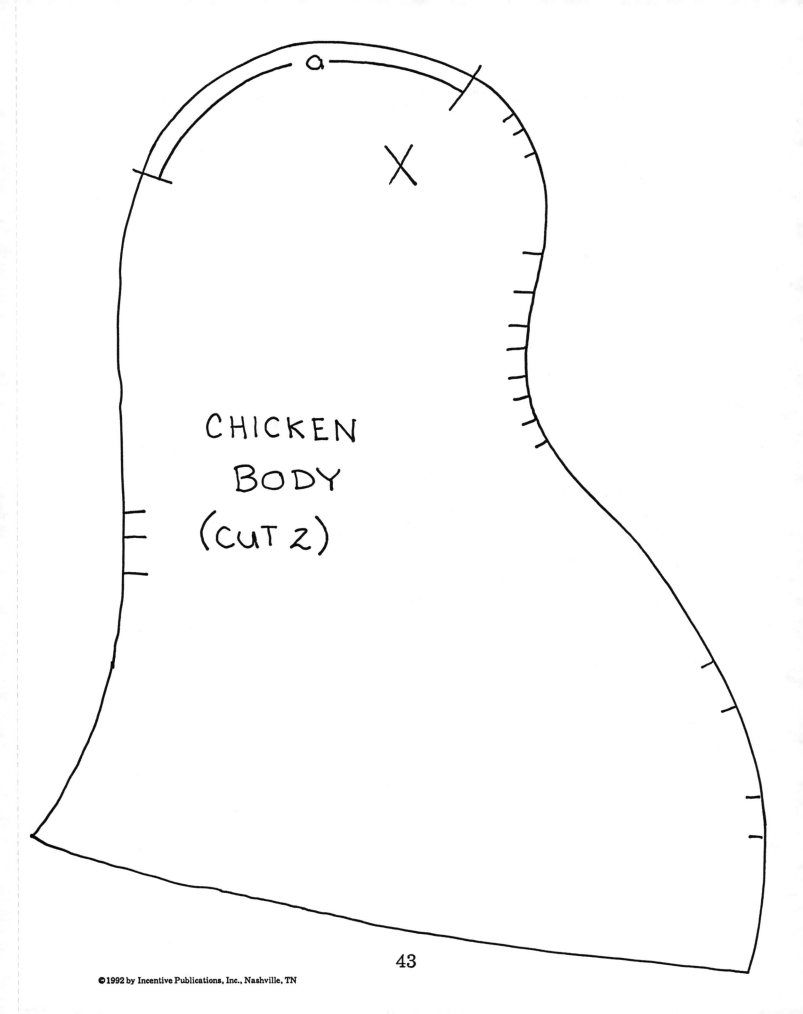

CHICKEN
BODY
(CUT 2)

43

# PERSONALITY PLUS
*Fabric Puppet*

## What To Use:

- ½ yard of colorful fabric
- needle and thread
- "scrap box goodies"
- tracing paper
- pencil
- scissors
- straight pins

## What To Do:

1. Cut out the patterns on the following pages.
2. Fold the fabric in half. Pin the dotted line on the front pattern along the fold line, and pin the back pattern beside it as shown.
3. Carefully cut out patterns along solid black lines. Make sure you do not cut along the fold line on the front pattern. You now have two back pieces and one front piece.
4. Pin right sides of the backs together and stitch along dotted line as shown on pattern piece. Open out and press.
5. Pin right side of front and right side of back together and stitch along dotted line. Turn puppet right side out and press.
6. If you need to hem the bottom edge of the puppet, turn fabric ¼ inch to the inside and stitch.
7. Decorate your fabric puppet with beads, braid, buttons, yarn, shells, nuts, and whatever other odds and ends you can find.

*Add wings and features to make Christmas angels or other winged creatures.*

44

OPTIONAL WING CUT 2

right sides together

FRONT
Cut 1

Place this edge on fold

46

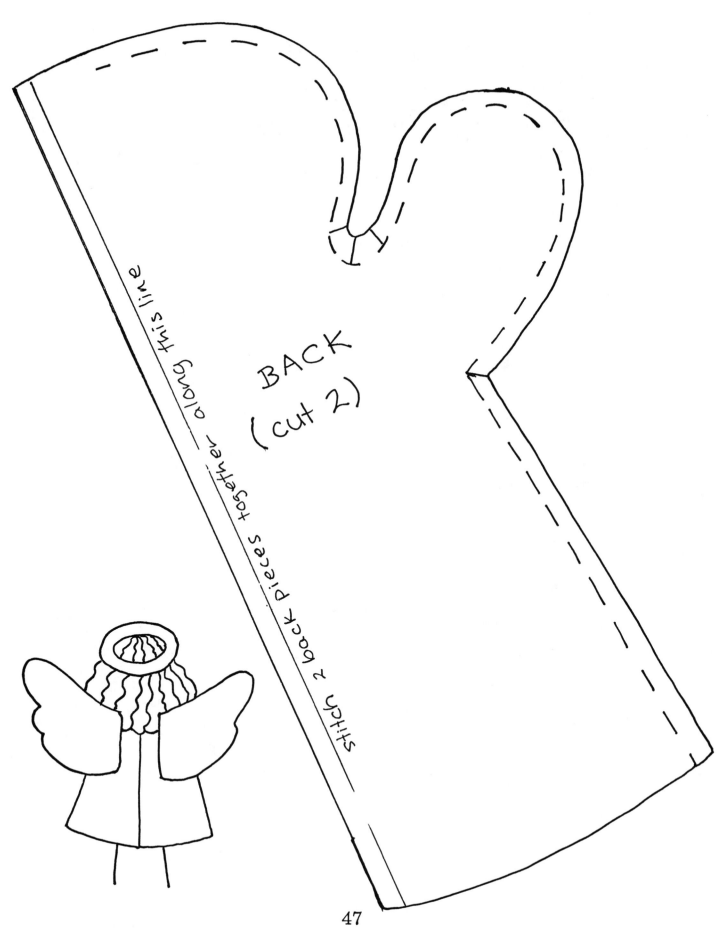

BACK
(cut 2)

stitch 2 back pieces together along this line

# DINOSAUR DOINGS

*Felt Hand Puppet*

## What To Use:

- yellow, orange, pink, white, and black felt
- light green yarn
- glue
- pencil
- scissors
- ½ yard of green felt

## What To Do:

1. Make a hand puppet from green felt (see Fabric Puppet on pages 44-47).

2. Cut two large circles from yellow felt for the paws, and paste them to the ends of the puppet's arms.

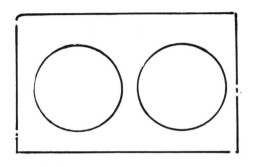

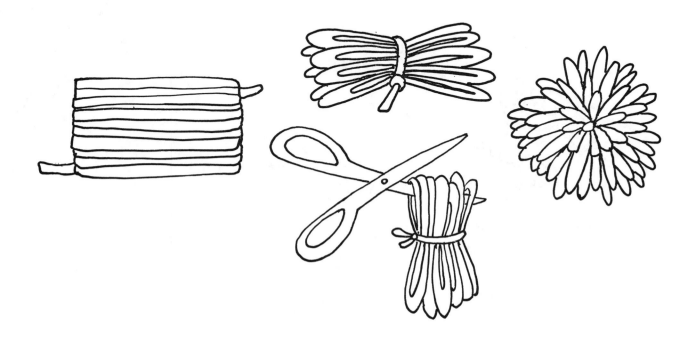

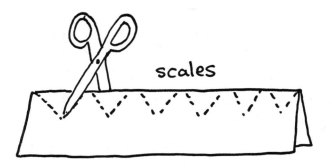

scales

eye

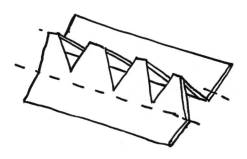

3. Make a green pompon by wrapping green yarn about 30 times around a 2-inch-wide card, sliding it off the card, and tying it tightly in the middle with a piece of yarn as shown. Cut out a black felt circle for the nose. Cut 2 to 4 teeth from white felt and cut out a pink felt tongue. Glue nose, teeth, and tongue to the pompon as shown.

4. To make the dinosaur's eyes, cut 2 ovals from yellow felt, 2 small circles from orange felt, and two smaller black felt circles for the pupils. Glue the pieces together as shown.

5. Cut two 1" circles of orange felt for cheeks and glue in place.

6. To make dinosaur scales, cut out a strip of orange triangles and glue it to the puppet's back as shown.

49

# LION ON THE LINE

*Felt Puppet*

## What To Use:

- pencil
- ½ yard yellow or gold felt
- smaller pieces of orange, pink, dark green, and dark yellow felt
- scissors
- glue
- yellow yarn

## What To Do:

1. Make a hand puppet from yellow or gold felt (see Fabric Puppet on pages 44-47).

2. To make paws, cut two large circles and six small circles from orange felt and glue them to the puppet's arms as shown.

3. Cut a nose from a triangle of pink felt. Make eyes by gluing two circles of dark yellow felt to two ovals of dark green felt. Glue nose and eyes to puppet's face.

4. Use the pattern to cut out the lion's mane: a large circle of dark yellow felt for the large mane, and a smaller circle of orange felt for the small mane. Fringe the ends of the mane as shown. Glue the center of the small mane to the back of the puppet's head. Then glue the center of the large mane to the center of the small mane.

5. Finish your lion puppet by making two small pompons from yellow yarn and gluing them under his nose. (To find out how to make a pompon, see page 49.)

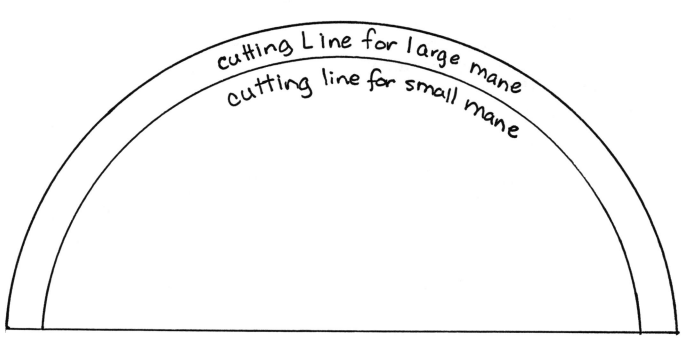

cutting Line for large mane

cutting line for small mane

51

# CREEPY CRAWLIES

*Shirt Sleeve Puppet*

## What To Use:

- old shirt sleeve
- needle and thread
- buttons
- felt
- scissors

## What To Do:

1. Cut off an old shirt sleeve at the elbow (or make it as long as the distance from your elbow to the end of your fist). Move the button so that the cuff will fit your forearm right below your elbow (see illustration).

2. Sew the cut end of the sleeve together with needle and thread. Sew on buttons for eyes, and sew on felt cutouts for mouth, nose, and ears.

*If you cut the sleeve long enough, you can make a mouth that will open and close by stuffing the sewn end of the sleeve back into the palm of your hand.*

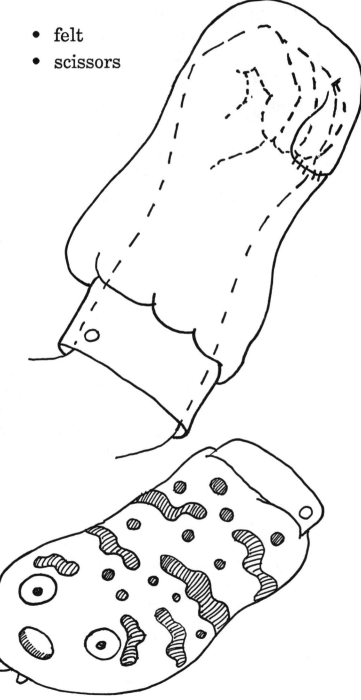

# ART SMART

# HAND IN HAND

*Whole Hand Puppets*

## What To Use:

- washable felt tip pens
- yarn
- cloth scraps or handkerchief

## What To Do:

1. Hold your hand lightly closed as shown. Look at your hand and think of a puppet character to create. To help you make this decision, move your thumb around to get the feel of a mouth opening and closing. Practice making the mouth talk, cough, laugh, and sing. Try wiggling your whole hand and your thumb at the same time.

2. Use washable felt tip pens to draw lips, eyes, and nose on your hand (or use Mom's old makeup). Add a moustache, beard, dimples, or freckles for interest. To get even fancier, you can use yarn or cloth to add a hat, hair, scarf, or ears.

# PAPER CAPER

*Construction Paper Puppet*

## What To Use:

- felt tip pens or crayons
- construction paper in a variety of colors
- scissors
- paste
- odd scraps

## What To Do:

1. Fold a piece of construction paper lengthwise into thirds. Then fold the paper in half, and then in half again as shown.

2. Stick your fingers in the top half and your thumb in the bottom half and open and close your puppet's mouth.

3. Use colored construction paper, felt tip pens, odd scraps, and pompons to give personality to your construction paper puppet.

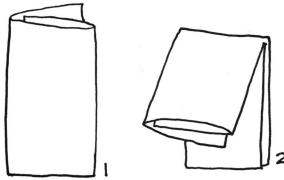

# YUM, YUM!

*Vegetable Puppet*

## What To Use:

- cloves, raisins, etc.
- knife
- vegetables such as bell pepper, squash, carrot, onion, etc.

## What To Do:

1. Pick a vegetable for the head of your puppet and wash and dry it thoroughly.

2. Select vegetable features to make a face for your puppet. Some ideas are: carrot circles for eyes, a raisin for a nose, bell pepper strips for hair—you may use whatever you have to make your vegetable puppet an edible delight.

eggplant

cut slits

cloves

carrot slices

baby carrot

lemon slice

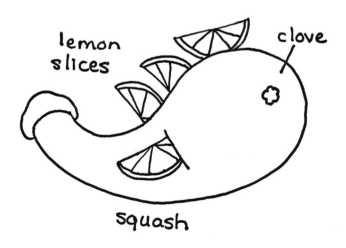

lemon slices

clove

squash

3. Use the knife to cut slits in the vegetable head, and slip the veggie features into the slits.

4. Insert a pencil or stick into the base of your puppet. Hold the pencil or stick to move the puppet around to create action.

5. Enjoy your vegetable creation. Vegetables are good for you!

# STOCKING SHOW

*Nylon Stocking Puppet*

## What To Use:

- 2 nylon stockings
- glue
- "scrap box goodies"
- scissors

## What To Do:

1. Cut one nylon stocking so that it covers your hand and forearm when you put your hand inside. The toe end of the stocking will be your puppet's head. Stuff the other stocking inside to give your puppet some shape.

2. Glue on "scrap box goodies" to decorate your stocking puppet.

3. Wiggle your hand between the two stockings to operate your puppet.

*Stocking puppets make great snakes or dragons.*

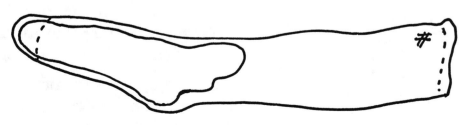

58

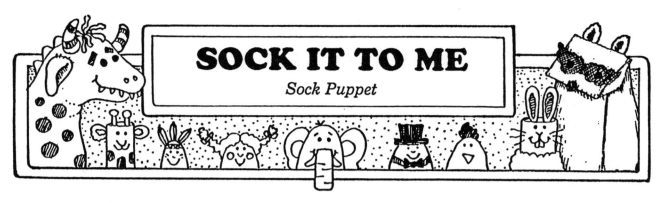

# SOCK IT TO ME

*Sock Puppet*

## What To Use:

- old sock
- felt tip pens
- scissors
- glue
- posterboard
- pencil

## What To Do:

1. Trace an oval around your hand as you rest it palm down on a piece of posterboard, as shown. Cut out the oval.

2. Fold the oval in half as shown and cover both inside flaps with glue. Turn the sock inside out and slip your hand inside it so your fingers are in the toe of the sock and the sock's heel goes over the back of your wrist. Place your sock-covered fingers in between the glued sides of the posterboard oval. Ask a friend to pull the sock off your hand and over the oval, turning the sock right side out. You should be able to see the "jaws" of the puppet now—make sure the inside fabric of the sock toe

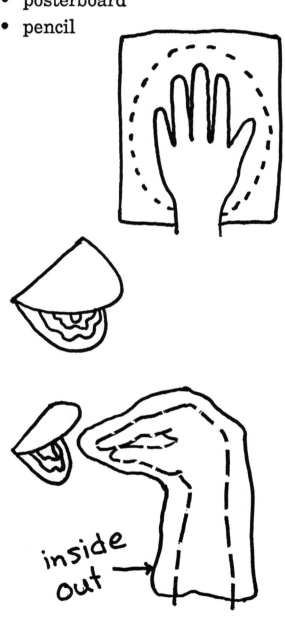

inside out

adheres smoothly to the glue-covered oval. The oval is an "invisible support" for the jaws.

3. Give your sock puppet some character by gluing on eyes, hair, horns, a hat, or whatever your imagination comes up with.

4. Place your hand inside the sock and move fingers and thumb to operate the sock puppet's jaw.

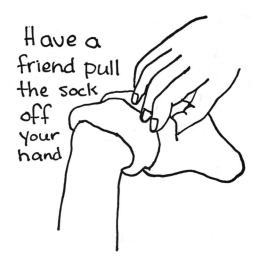

Have a friend pull the sock off your hand

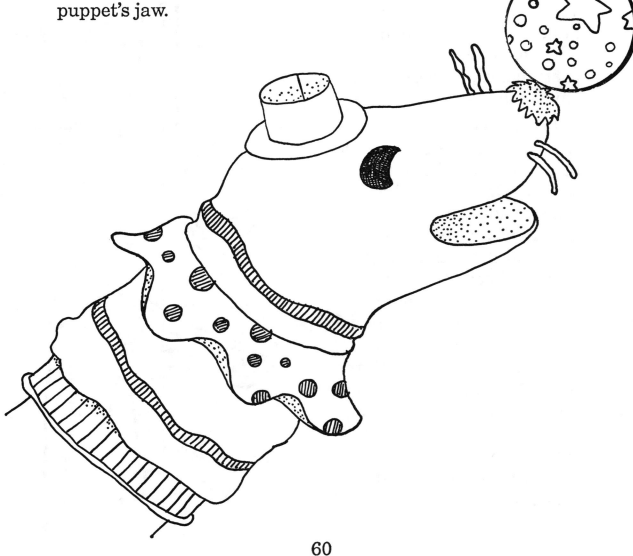

# BALL CALL
## *Ball Puppet*

**What To Use:**

- tennis ball or styrofoam ball
- paring knife or scissors
- felt tip pens
- cloth handkerchief
- string

**What To Do:**

1. With scissors or knife, gouge out a hole in the ball. The hole should be about an inch deep and wide enough for your second finger.

2. Use felt tip pens to make a face on the ball. Add hair, ears, or a crown of paper if you like.

3. Drape the handkerchief over your hand as shown and push your handkerchief-covered second finger into the hole in the ball. Your thumb and your little finger are the ball puppet's arms. To help define the "arms," tie a loose piece of string around each one.

61

# ANI-MULE!

*Paper-Strip-And-Tissue-Roll Puppet*

## What To Use:

- newspaper or paper towel strips
- wheat or wallpaper paste
- tape or string
- toilet tissue rolls
- tempera paint
- paintbrush
- varnish or clear acrylic medium

## What To Do:

1. Cover your work space with newspapers or other protective materials.

2. Tape or tie together cardboard rolls from toilet tissue to make an interesting form—a monster, an animal, a space creature, or whatever you like.

3. Mix the paste with cold water until it is of a thin, creamy consistency. Stir well to make sure all the lumps disappear.

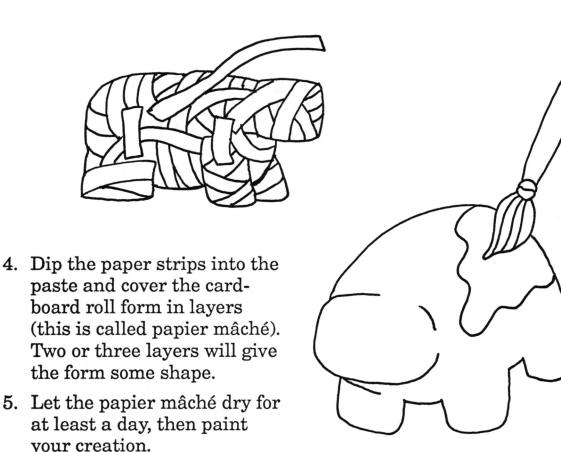

4. Dip the paper strips into the paste and cover the cardboard roll form in layers (this is called papier mâché). Two or three layers will give the form some shape.

5. Let the papier mâché dry for at least a day, then paint your creation.

6. After the paint has dried, add a coat of varnish or clear acrylic medium to make your puppet shine. You may add hair or other decorations to complete your papier mâché puppet. A pencil or stick can be inserted into your "Ani-Mule" to use as a handle.

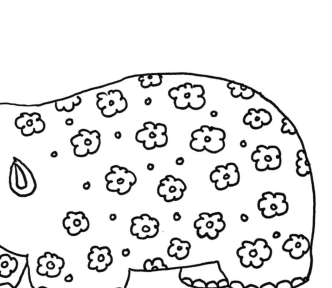

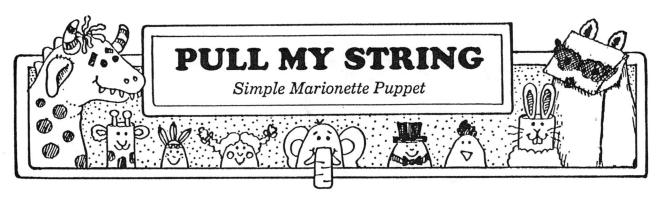

## What To Use:

- crayons or felt tip pens
- 2 brads
- string
- scissors

## What To Do:

1. Color the clown pattern on the following page, then carefully cut it out.

2. Punch out the holes on the clown's arms and body with the scissors. Attach the arms to the body with the brads.

3. Use the scissors to make holes at the end of each clown hand and at the top of the clown's hat. Attach a piece of string to each hole. Make a slipknot at the other end of each piece of string, as shown.

4. To operate your marionette, slip your thumb and little finger through the slipknots at the ends of the clown's hand strings, and put your index finger through the knot of the string attached to the clown's hat. Make your puppet dance and move!

64

# IN THE BAG

*Paper Bag Puppet*

## What To Use:

- brown paper bag
- construction paper
- paste
- felt tip pens
- scissors

## What To Do:

1. Fold the bottom of the bag flat against one side to make the space for your hand, as shown.

2. Choose patterns from the following three pages, and use them to cut construction paper features to paste on the paper bag.

3. Use felt tip pens to decorate your paper bag puppet and make it more colorful and exciting.

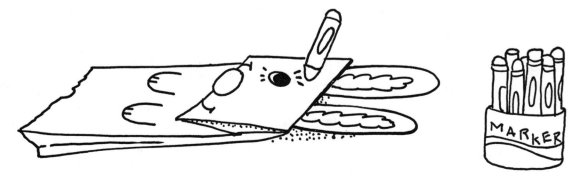

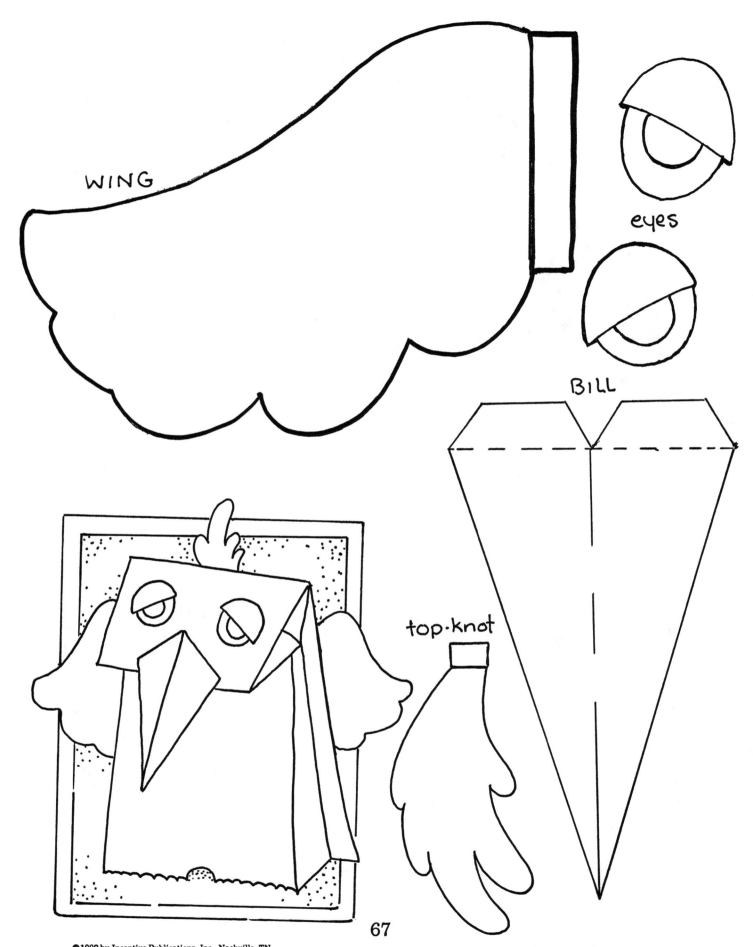

WING

eyes

BILL

top-knot

67

NOSE

MASK

EARS

TAIL

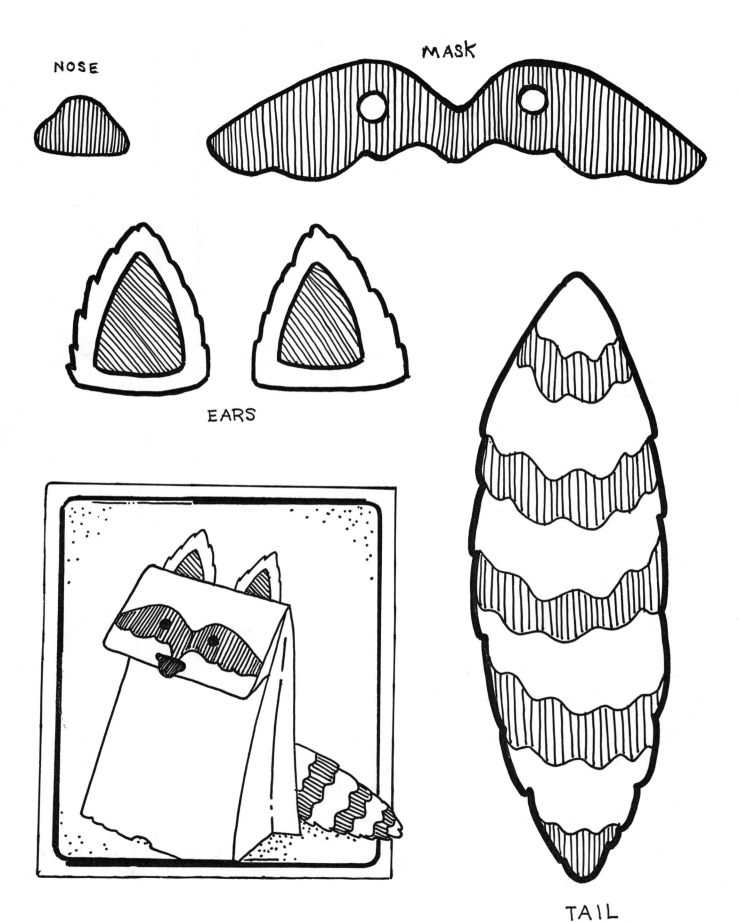

68

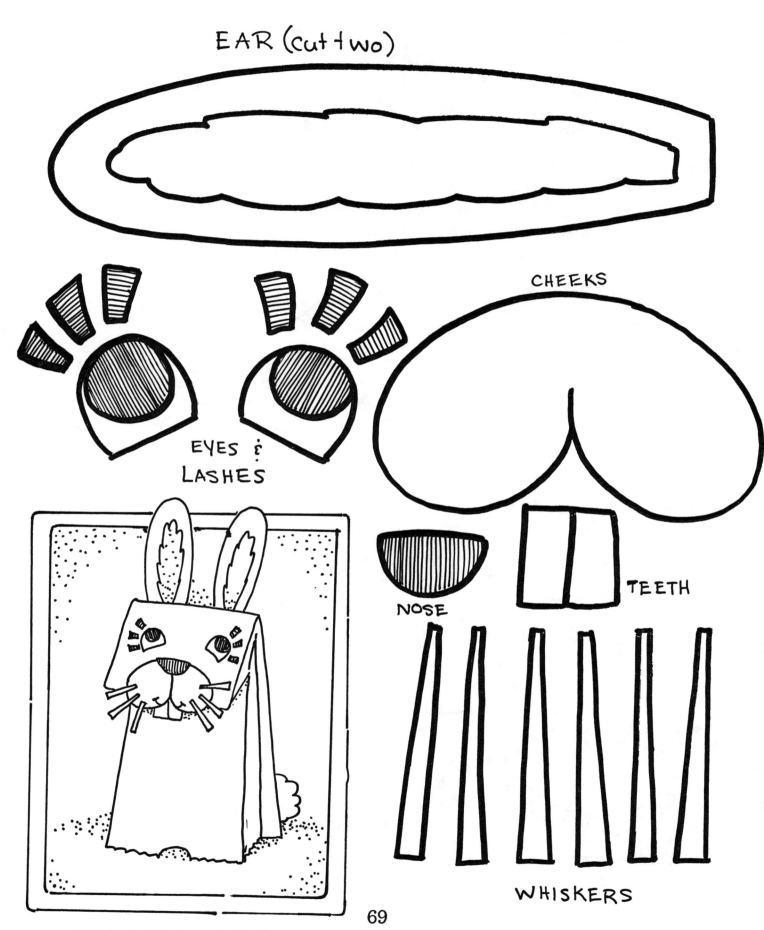

EAR (cut two)

CHEEKS

EYES &
LASHES

NOSE

TEETH

WHISKERS

69

# PASTE UP
## Puppet Parts To Paste

Select some of the features on this page to make a paper bag puppet. Color the chosen features, cut them out, and paste them to a small brown paper bag. Name your puppet and write a play for it.

*A friend can use the leftovers to make a companion for your puppet. Write a play together for your two puppets.*

# APPENDIX

# TEACHING TIPS FOR USING PUPPETS

Puppets can be used in the classroom to teach, reteach, drill, motivate, introduce new concepts, or just to entertain.

Use puppet or puppets to:

- introduce a new child to the group. The puppet can tell some special things about the new child in order to encourage the other children to want to get acquainted.

- present health tips to a group, using questions asked by the puppet and answered by the children.

- tell stories in the first person (the puppet may be the main character of the story).

- lead group singing.

- lead a spelling bee.

- introduce children to various handicaps that cannot be explained easily using real people (blindness, deafness, cerebral palsy).

- help build an awareness of other cultures. Each child could make a puppet representing a different country.

- reinforce positive self-concepts. Children could make puppets of themselves and act out various feelings, attitudes, and opinions regarding important issues.

- explore the career world. Puppets could role play "employer and employee" and practice interviewing and filling out applications.

- provide incentives for creative writing endeavors by individual students or cooperative learning teams.

- reinforce positive group interaction skills and good manners by role playing.

- demonstrate safety awareness and anti-drug consciousness behavior.

- present ecological and environmental issues.

72

# PUPPET PERSONALITIES

All of the puppets in this book can be given interesting features and faces using construction paper, felt, buttons, trims from the scrap box, and felt tip pens. Along the way, each puppet will acquire a personality and character all its own.

Choose one of the following traits or moods to show on the face of a puppet you create.

silly

clever
stupid
hungry
witty

serious
happy
grateful
snobbish

surprised

sad
funny
silly
scared
sleepy
lazy

snobbish

humble
tricky
modern
surprised
old-fashioned
mysterious

bored
excited
smart
peaceful
nervous
interested
confused

confused

mysterious

*Give your puppets names that describe their personalities.*

# "MADE BY YOU" STAGES

Any puppet play is more interesting when you use your imagination and surprise your audience by presenting your play from an original "made by you" stage.

Clever stages are not as hard to make as you may think. As a matter of fact, you may find some "ready-to-use" stages just waiting to become part of a puppet play.

Have you thought about using . . .

- a table turned on its side. Work from behind the tabletop as the puppets perform along the upturned edge.

- a card table with a sheet or blanket draped over if. You work from behind the table and use the tabletop as your stage.

- an overturned chair. This will work if you need a stage in a hurry and there is nothing else around. Drape a coat or shawl over the chair and kneel down behind it.

- a tablecloth tacked or taped across a doorway. Ask your audience to sit on the opposite side of the door as you hide behind the tablecloth and hold your puppets above the cloth.

- two chairs with a board placed between them. Cover the board with an old sheet that touches the floor and you will have a super stage behind which several people can work.

- a windowsill where the audience can sit on one side of the window and you on the other. This works especially well if you have a windowshade that can be raised or lowered to give you a "stage curtain."

- an old tablecloth between two trees. This will work for an outside stage.

- a low bush. Kneel behind it and use the top of the bush for the stage.

- an upturned shoebox with one side cut out. This makes a great stage for finger puppets.

- a shallow box top with two holes cut for your hands to fit through. This will make a fine stage for a "traveling" puppet show. Just fasten sturdy string to the four corners so that the box top will hang from your neck. Stick your hands through the holes, put the puppets on your hands—and on with the show! This is a good way to use a puppet show for party entertainment or to announce special events in classrooms or to family members.

- three sides of a refrigerator box, set up vertically, and with a rectangle cut out of the middle side for the stage opening.

# LIGHTING, SOUND EFFECTS, COSTUMES

The right lighting, sound effects, and costumes can really help to make your puppet play believable. Here are some suggestions for simple ways to make your play come alive.

## Lighting

- flashlight
- nightlight
- lamp with shade removed
- penlight
- candle
- hurricane lamp
- overhead projector
- filmstrip projector

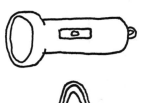

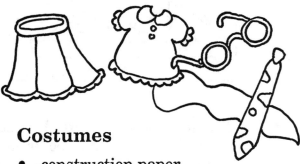

## Costumes

- construction paper
- old doll clothes
- cut-up pillowcases colored with felt tip pens
- glasses/sunglasses
- hats
- net
- pipe cleaners
- dishcloths
- bandanna
- old jewelry
- scarves
- lampshade
- paper bag
- ties
- boxes
- tagboard

## Sound Effects

- playing musical instruments
- shoes striking a hard surface
- clapping hands
- firmly closing a book
- rasping a fingernail against sandpaper
- stirring rocks in aluminum pie pan
- blowing a whistle
- playing taped or recorded music
- closing doors
- rattling dishes
- crinkling paper

*All of the above sounds can be recorded and played for a special play!*

# RHYMES AND SONGS FOR PUPPET ACTION

| SONG/RHYME | PUPPET CHARACTERS | PROPS |
|---|---|---|
| Little Boy Blue | Little Boy Blue, sheep, cow | horn, haystack, cornstalks |
| A Frog Went A Courting | Frog, Uncle Rat, Miss Mouse, Tom Cat, Bumble Bee, Miss Flea, Mistress Rat | food, drinks, saddle and bridle |
| Old King Cole | Old King Cole, Three Fiddlers | pipe, bowl, fiddles |
| Little Bo-Peep | Little Bo-Peep, sheep | crook, sheep's tails, handkerchief |
| Frère Jacques | Brother John, bell ringer | bed, bell |
| Rock-A-Bye, Baby | baby | tree, cradle |
| Jingle Bells | children, horse | sleigh, bells |
| Round The Mulberry Bush | boys and girls | none (actions can be carried on without props) |
| Oats, Peas, Beans, And Barley grow | farmer, wife | none |
| The Farmer In The Dell | farmer, wife, child, nurse, dog, cat, rat, cheese | none |
| A Tisket, A Tasket | girl, little boy | basket, letter |
| Round The Village | boy, girl | house with windows big enough for puppets to go through (could be made from a shoebox) |
| The Eency Weency Spider | spider, sun | water spout, something to make the sound of rain |

# DO:

- **Do** think about the puppet you want to make before you begin working. If you are using written directions or suggestions, read them all the way through very carefully. If you are making a creative puppet from your own idea, make a sketch to work from.

- **Do** gather all the needed supplies and equipment *before* you begin work.

- **Do** read directions on glue, paint and other containers, and follow all the safety instructions.

- **Do** keep your work space neat and orderly when working.

- **Do** clean up and put your supplies away when finished.

- **Do** try to add your own creative touch to every puppet you make so that it will be truly "yours."

# DON'T:

- **Don't** rush to finish a puppet. Take all the time you need to let glue or paste dry thoroughly before you begin the next step.

- **Don't** use glue, paint or other permanently drying supplies without covering your work surface with newspaper.

- **Don't** use other people's supplies without asking permission (even if you need only a tiny bit).

- **Don't** use buttons, beads or other hard objects on puppets to be used by small children. (They can come off and be dangerous to small children.)

- **Don't** use scissors, knives, or other sharp objects without first checking with an adult. Always remember to hold these tools away from your body as you work, and use cutting motions away from your body.

# INDEX